The Legend of
Morgan's Corner
and Other Ghost Stories
of Hawai'i

The Legend of
Morgan's Corner
and Other Ghost Stories
of Hawai'i

Lopaka Kapanui

Mutual Publishing

Copyright © 2006 by Mutual Publishing

Library of Congress Cataloging-in-Publication Data

Kapanui, Lopaka.
  The legend of Morgan's Corner and other ghost stories of Hawai'i / Lopaka Kapanui.
      p. cm.
  Summary: "A collection of ghost stories from Hawaii"--Provided by publisher.
   ISBN-13: 978-1-56647-792-5 (pbk. : alk. paper)
   ISBN-10: 1-56647-792-1 (pbk. : alk. paper)
  1. Ghosts--Hawaii. 2. Legends--Hawaii. I. Title.
  BF1472.U6K37 2006
  133.109969--dc22

                              2006016652

ISBN-10: 1-56647-792-1
ISBN-13: 978-1-56647-792-5

Cover art by Roy Chang
Design by Jane Gillespie

First Printing, September 2006
1 2 3 4 5 6 7 8 9

Mutual Publishing, LLC
1215 Center Street, Suite 210
Honolulu, Hawaii 96816
Ph: (808) 732-1709
Fax: (808) 734-4094
e-mail: mutual@mutualpublishing.com
www.mutualpublishing.com

Printed in Taiwan

Dedication

To Glen Grant and all the tellers of stories who have unselfishly handed down the knowledge of our people's history—supernatural, personal or otherwise. Some choose to languish in their grief for the dearly departed. I choose to continue their legacy by telling their stories, thereby, keeping them alive and constantly among us.

Table of Contents

Acknowledgments

To my wife, Marguerite. Of all the goals I have set for myself, your happiness is at the top of the list. I love you. To our daughter, Hiwalani. There was a moment in the past when your mother and I had exhausted every possible way of expressing our love for each other. Finally, when our love became as pure as the faith of a child, you were created. Nine months later, you were given to us. Our love for you is immeasurable and inexhaustable, never doubt that this is true. To my Aunty Lani Kapanui, my Mother Angie, Aunty Rosie, Aunty Kalua, Uncle Joe, Uncle Vince, and Uncle Victor. It is my hope that this humble work has brought pride and honor to the Kapanui name. If this is so, then Kopa and Annie Pimoe (Grandpa and Grandma) must be smiling down upon us.

To Mr. Robert Abuel, thank you for the bowl of light. To Sandra and James Vidad, thank you for your support and faith. To Eric, for introducing me to the sinful pleasures of Denny's ultimate omelette!

To my kumu hula, Kula Abiva. My mahalo for your steadfast patience and faith.

To Robert Pennybacker, aren't you glad that you're in the acknowledgements and not having to write the introduction at the last minute? I love you brother, thanks. To Don Wilson, Scott Warraca, Norman Ipson, Charley Wegner, Jack Hughes, the late Warren Stremming, Raymond Wiekoweicz, Jr., Keaka Hashimoto, Jacob Leong, Charley Stevens and Marc Rubenstein, John Connell, and John Topliss, my brothers of Ko'olau Lodge. Thank you for all of your support during the best and worst of times.

To Wailani Robins, for weaving this Lei of Aloha and being the tie which binds us all.

To Jeff Gere for being cool. To the leaders and members of the Sokka Gakkai who consistently provide the means to always follow the correct path of faith. Nam Myo Ho Renge Kyo!

Lastly, 'ia 'oe e ku'u 'Ululani, for providing 'ike that the 'iwa was more than just a bird, he was a fierce chiefly warrior who did not lash the backs of his people, but darkened his own, by working along side them, thereby, earning their love and respect.

Now, to the seen and the unseen. I ask your permission to open this feast of knowledge and give it protection, provide this table with love, and see that all who have come here are returned home safely to their loved ones.

Introduction

Since the publication of my first book, *Haunted Hawaiian Nights,* I've had a recurring dream. In it, I am standing on the large, spacious front porch of 'Iolani Palace. It is midday, and the sun is directly overhead, casting no shadow.

The pathway to the gate which leads out to King Street—the Kauikeaouli gate—is lined with torches, which burn brightly even in the noonday sun. In times past, they were a symbol of King Kalākaua's kapu status.

In my dream, I can see that the palace grounds and the streets are filled with people, restless and eager, waiting for something to happen. But there is no state occasion or holiday, or royal proclamation. Then I look again, and I see that the people have no faces.

I am seized by fear and wish to run back into the safety of the palace, but someone is blocking the tall double doors. It is my mentor and friend, Glen Grant.

He is dressed in a gray double-breasted jacket, pleated pants, and a matching fedora, and he seems as impassive as McDougal, the fictional detective he created. But then I see him smile, seeing the terror in my face, and I feel his hand on my shoulder. "They're waiting for you," he says quietly. "Speak to them. They need to hear your voice. Anything. A word, a sentence, a phrase. Anything at all."

And I hiss at him under my breath, "They're all faceless ghosts!" Ignoring my protests, Glen pushes me gently toward the top of the palace steps. I look back at him for reassurance, but he is gone. And, for the first time in my life I am at a loss for words.

Here the dream ends.

The dream, I thought, might have been the result of all the ghost stories and the tours of haunted places that I do for a living. And maybe one of them—a woman without a face I'll tell you about in this book—hacked her way into my subconscious mind, like a computer virus.

Then again, the dream began right after my first work was published. It was dedicated to Glen, and those of you lucky enough to have accompanied him on his tours know that he explored 'Iolani Palace. And I was his student. And here the dream begins to make sense, because Glen was the sort of guy who would always push me gently, firmly forward. But the faceless crowd still puzzles me.

Perhaps the faceless people in my dream are not ghosts at all, but you—my readers,

And perhaps I'm meeting you for the first time—or maybe a second time, for those of you who read my first book—and when I do, your faces will appear. It makes as much sense as anything. Of course, you can never be too sure about dreams, but you never know. I hope these stories entertain and instruct you.

Aloha mai kāua!

I am Lopaka Kapanui, and I invite you to read on.

Döppelgangers

This story is as much Glen's as mine, perhaps even more so, and I'm going to start the book with it.

The first thing you need to know is that Glen's love and respect for our culture, history, legends, and religion was both genuine and boundless. And we loved him and his work without reservation.

Some of you may remember a controversy concerning a movie about Kamehameha I. The star of the movie was to be a non-Hawaiian. We were talking about it one day, and, out of the blue, Glen asked me, "You know the only way this movie will work?"

I was stumped. The only thing I knew was that no matter how well the movie was made, there would be trouble.

"It would work," Glen explained, "only if the story was told from the viewpoint of John Young. That's the only way Hollywood and the public would accept it."

John Young was Kamehameha's most trusted friend. Surprisingly, he was a haole sailor, but history, like politics, makes for strange bedfellows.

I'd almost forgotten the conversation; we'd gone on to other things. The other day, though, I wandered into a Native Hawaiian bookstore. After browsing a bit, I saw a picture of Glen on the wall, a portrait. I'd never seen it before. As I approached it, I saw that he was wearing a missionary outfit—a black vest and billowy white sleeves. I stepped even closer; the plaque appeared to have Glen's name on it. But as I squinted closely, I saw the name "John Young."

Try it sometime, if you have a chance. Take any picture of Glen up close. Then look at John Young's. And you can draw your own conclusions.

'Ekolu Mea Nui

Before we go any further, let's look at the world we're trying to discover. Remember this, first of all: there are ghosts, and there are two kinds of spirits. A ghost was once a human being. Because of the circumstances surrounding that person's death, he or she is bound to the earth, unable to move on. This applies generally to sudden or tragic deaths, or to people who love the place in which they lived so much that they cannot quite leave it.

A ghost has no sense of time or of its own surroundings. When you see a ghost, you are often seeing what it believes to be its normal, everyday routine. It is usually unaware of your presence; if it does see you, it thinks you're the ghost.

People often say that they feel the air change before they see a ghost. The atmosphere becomes suddenly colder, even frigid. This is because the ghost, in becoming visible, needs to absorb heat from the air. If there is not enough available heat, it has a couple of options. It can take the form of an orb, or a small ball of light. It can also absorb other sources of heat—electrical equipment, cameras, light bulbs, car engines, and flashlights.

▼ ▼ ▼

Then there are the spirits—simply put, good ones and bad ones. The good spirits are easy to describe, and a delight. They represent people who have been dead for a long time, and who return now and again to visit, often to provide silent and invisible comfort.

The bad spirits are something else again. You see, they were never real human beings to begin with, and had no previous incarnation in flesh and blood. And they are attracted to specific kinds of people. If you don't want to find out who they are, stop right here. Go on to the stories.

▼ ▼ ▼

OK, you've been warned. These spirits are attracted to people who have low opinions of themselves and little or no confidence, or those who complain constantly, offering nothing nice to say. They are attracted to people with a lot of emotional baggage—who are no longer children but not quite adults. Or, sometimes, people with severe emotional conflicts. When these spirits sense someone with these traits, they are like sharks spotting blood in the water. Except for that the sharks' work is quick. The bad spirits attach themselves to people, follow them home, and wait.

They wait for nightfall, and appear in the darkness of bedrooms—shadows darker than anything imaginable. The people I've met who have seen these shadows say that when you shine a light on them, they simply consume the light. Nothing passes through them.

Then they crawl into bed with their prey and slowly begin to choke them in a way that is ritualistic. They begin with fingers around the back of the neck. Then they slowly press both thumbs down on the Adams' apple. They keep pressing until they are sure—in a way only spirits can be sure—that they have killed. And then they let go.

To compound the terror, people who are choked by bad spirits are awake all the time, able to see, hear and feel everything. But they are suddenly and inexplicably paralyzed.

There is, of course, a scientific explanation for all this—one known commonly as sleep paralysis.

But there's another explanation as well. According to a Sanskrit translation of a Mahayana sutra, the choking ghost may be the result of something known as karmic sickness. This sutra says that in previous lifetimes, one has done some terrible things, and brought negative energy into the world. If one's karma does not change from lifetime to lifetime, there is an accumulation of negative energy, and the soul is stuck like a clogged sink.

When the spirits become too strong to resist, there is danger for everyone. People have been known to commit murder under their influence.

Psychics and parapsychologists will always advise you that before entering a graveyard or any haunted place, you must first offer a prayer or ask permission. For reasons not yet known, the spirits honor these requests; indeed, they must even provide protection. Be careful, though, in your choice of companions. If your companion acts foolish or flippant, all bets are off.

I've given you some idea of what we face in that part of the world we cannot see. Good luck, and read on.

Don't Panic!

The tall trees on Morgan's Corner on Kiona'ole Road cover the road like a cathedral, and on a dark night, they are ominous and beautiful. They block out all light, and it is nearly impossible to see one's hand in front of one's face. It is a dark and moody place, one in which it might be easy, and unwise, to panic.

Last Halloween, I led an investigation there for some corporate types from Radio Shack and AT&T. They were eager, festively dressed in costumes, full of hope and excitement. But the rain began falling with no letup, and soon everyone was miserable. We couldn't visit the usual sites; the land was drenched with water and mud. But we decided to see Morgan's Corner, and were pleasantly surprised to find that the rain had not touched the Ko'olau side of the island at all; the weather was clear. But as we approached Morgan's Corner this time, it seemed unusually dark and forbidding. Something just didn't feel right. Before we walked up the road, I suddenly decided to warn the group. I stopped.

"Don't panic," I said, quietly and firmly. "The road is dark, and you won't even be able to see your hands in front of your faces. Above all, don't let your imaginations get the better of you. No matter what happens, or what you may hear, see or feel, don't panic."

They agreed mutely, and prepared to enter the forest. The forest, some say, is guarded by a haunted tree, and I make it a point to stop, and silently ask its permission to enter. As I did so, there was a horrible crash. It was loud, like thunder, and came from nowhere.

And, of course, they panicked. A woman dressed like Raggedy Ann turned around, pushed her husband to the ground and stepped on his head. A man in a G.I. Joe uniform screamed like a woman and ran around in circles. Three teenaged girls, dressed as seductive nurses, turned around and ran over a man six feet six inches tall. And someone ran past me, managing to knock the spotlight out of my hands, breaking it at the handle.

A man about five feet tall jumped over an eight-foot fence. And the poor driver on the opposite side of the fence screamed and ran off when he saw a ghost with orange hair and a clown's face, shrieking like a banshee.

When you lead a group into a haunted forest, you have to remember that you wear a sign that says, "The Buck Stops Here." Most of the time I'm the good guy, but sometimes I've got to be the bad guy. Once everyone was on the bus, I told them we had to get out and find the source of the mayhem. I did it as much for myself as for them. I don't mind the inexplicable, as long as I can say I didn't run away from it. Reluctantly, everyone got out of the bus with a collective moan.

I still had a flashlight, and as we headed toward the forest again, we saw a branch that had fallen from maybe fifteen feet up, crashing through the other branches and hitting the road.

"There's your ghost," I said. "A branch."

Raggedy Ann said "Yeah, but isn't that a branch from the haunted tree?" I looked carefully. She was right. I nodded.

"And when the branch from that tree hits the ground, aren't there restless spirits still sitting on it?" She was right again, and I nodded and said, "Yeah," very cool. But I felt a chill at the base of my spine.

"So," said Raggedy Ann, "if the branch hit the ground with all those restless spirits on it, where are they now?"

The chill in my back had reached my neck, and for the first time since I was a kid, I screamed like a woman. It wasn't a pretty sound. I try not to think about it too much.

We've Only Just Begun

I've talked about Morgan's Corner a lot in this book. But I guess I haven't really told you how I feel about it, because I really don't know myself. It is, I guess, part Grail, part ghost, friend, adversary, practical joker, shrine, the beginning of the world and the end. Whatever it is for me, it's the final, crucial way station for the people I lead—a proving ground for the faithful and the doubtful alike. So I still take people there, and always know that somehow, Morgan's Corner will prove itself again and again.

During one journey, there were two guys in the group. One was an old man, a complete skeptic, a disbeliever I dubbed Doubting Thomas. The other was a psychic named Eric. He and I would become fast friends. But I'm ahead of the story.

It was September, as I remember, though I'm not sure of the year. On the bus, Doubting Thomas kept ribbing me. "You're full of it, you know," he'd say, but he was so good-natured I shrugged it off. We visited the usual sites, and finally got to

Morgan's Corner. He leaped out of the bus so that he could be the first to hug the haunted tree. He yelled out, "This'll *prove* it. You're full of beans. All *shibai.*"

Satisfied, he let go of the tree and began walking back toward me. "See?" he said, "I told you you were full of..." and suddenly he fell flat on his face, with a high-pitched scream—a woman's scream, shrill and piercing.

"It's got me!" he yelled desperately. "It's got me! Help!"

We crowded around him and found his pants leg caught on some barbed wire that had been somehow, inexplicably, wrapped around the tree trunk. I stifled a laugh. Everyone else seemed merely annoyed, and said nothing, shaking their heads, snorting and smirking. I cut the wire, and he walked away, slowly. He didn't say anything else that night. Not a word. Come to think of it, I didn't say much either.

But before we left, Eric leaned over to me and in a conspiratorial whisper said, "There was a young girl standing just up the road there, watching us all the time. Did you know she was murdered here?"

"I know," I told him. "I know the story."

"She's not done," he said.

I drew a breath. "Not done with me, anyway."

"You're right," he said.

Doubting Thomas and I were the quietest ones on the bus that night, and Eric didn't say much either. And that's the end of the story. Morgan's Corner is a place beyond and above words and indifferent to them. What I did know was that I would eventually discover its legend, and that it would either make me a wise man or destroy me completely.

Yesterday Once More

Her name was Dana Bonafacio, and no one noticed her until she went missing. My own memory of that day is a bit hazy; I remember that it was sometime in July of '01, and I'd been hired to take a group out on investigation—Malihini Electric Company, I think it was—employees, family members. It was a long night. We made five stops, and as I told ghost stories at each one, it seemed that Dana was in the crowd, listening intensely. She didn't talk to anyone and didn't ask any questions.

Our last stop was at Morgan's Corner, and I sat in the jump seat next to Tolentino, our driver. A young woman was calling my name, and as I turned around, I saw her waving her arms wildly. Then she bolted from her seat and headed toward me. "Turn around! Turn around! We forgot somebody!" She kept waving her hands, and I had to believe her, but I tried to calm her. "Who did we forget?" I asked. This made her angry.

"Are you serious?" she yelled at me. "Look, I know you do all this to scare people, but this is cruel!" I was confused, and her anger turned to fury.

"Are you serious?" she screamed, over and over again. "The girl is missing!"

I was getting jumpy myself, but I tried not to show it. "I've got no idea who you're talking about. What girl?"

"Oh, my God!" she hissed, in a tone of utter disbelief. "You are serious. You don't know who I'm talking about?"

I managed a kind, wan smile, and said, "Seriously. I have no idea." Her sigh was one of angry resignation, and made me feel like the stupidest man on earth.

In a calm manner which she barely controlled, she spoke to me as a parent might to a wayward child. "She must have been five feet tall or so, maybe thirteen years old. Hapa-haole girl, long, reddish—auburn hair, and she parted it down the middle. She had rectangular wire glasses—you know—the kind our parents wore when they were in high school?"

I nodded in mute agreement, never having known what kind of glasses any of our parents wore back then.

"She was standing between me and my sister the whole night, every stop. The only time I missed her was when we stopped for a bite to eat. But back there at Morgan's Corner, when you were telling stories, she stood between my sister and me again. I think she had fallen down or something."

I was still dazed, and the fatigue of the trip didn't help. "What do you mean, fallen down?"

"Look, I saw her. The whole left side of her face was covered with dirt and mud, and there was some on her knees and thighs. Then the moon began to shine through the trees above us. Remember?"

"Yes," I replied. "I certainly remember that."

"And it kind of lit up the whole area, remember?" I nodded, trying to be judicious, a sage advising a troubled and testy pilgrim.

"Well, when I looked at her again, I saw it wasn't mud or dirt. She had black and blue bruises, and her knees and thighs were skinned or something. It kinda looked like somebody had dragged her across the road on her knees."

That one took a while to register. All I could manage to say was, "Terrible. My God, that's terrible." And the anger in her swelled up again, her eyes bulging like bullets. "Well turn this bus around, for Chrissake! We've gotta get her! She's hurt!"

What I hadn't realized is that Tolentino had already turned the bus around in the middle of our argument. I reached over gently, on an impulse, and put my hand on his arm. "Stop the bus," I said.

The bus came to a gradual halt. Tolentino, a

great guy but emotional and superstitious, began pounding his head on the steering wheel and began praying out loud in a wail. The inside of the bus was quiet; its thirty-eight seats might as well have been empty. I looked at the girl and, very quietly, asked her, "Before we go any further, do me a favor."

"What?" she screamed. "What now?"

"Turn around," I said, as calmly as I could, "and tell me if you see any empty seats on this bus."

She turned slowly, then began to shake and wail, as she struggled for words. "Oh-my-God-there! Ai-aisle seat on the right! Right there! That's her seat! Right there!"

The silence in the bus had turned into silent fear; I could feel it, and cursed my folly. Of course everyone had heard the conversation. And they could hear Tolentino, still praying and oblivious. And then I thought, hell, this is a joke. I'll go back there, and someone will pop out from under the seat and say, "Gotcha!" Then I thought again, coldly and logically. "No, sweetheart." I said, feeling tired, irritable, and condescending. "That's *your* seat. No one like that has been on this tour the entire night. I don't know who you're talking about. I haven't seen her, and it's my business to know everyone by sight."

I asked Tolentino, very gently, if he'd start the bus again, and he nodded. We headed back to town, and the mood of the bus was one of uneasy relief. For as I walked up and down the aisles, the other thirty-seven passengers gave me the same description as the young woman had. For them, she was someone else. She hadn't come with any of them. It was pretty clear to me that they were shaken, bewildered, or both, but as we approached Ward Avenue, the familiar lights of the city seemed to reassure most of them, and some even fell asleep before we got home.

▼ ▼ ▼

There's a term we use to explain improbable plots in books and movies: the willing suspension of disbelief. Go along with me on this one, because I'm still trying to figure it out myself. For some reason, I'd known the name of a girl I'd never seen. Thirty-eight others had seen her. And yet, somehow, the odds were tipped in my favor, a long shot, a minority of one.

All this happened on a Friday, and Dana was with me through the weekend. I got through Monday just fine. I remember ironing my clothes when the six o'clock news came on. I heard the newscaster say "Kiona'ole Road." Kiona'ole Road is also called Morgan's Corner. I nearly dropped the iron. The newscaster was brisk, and continued:

"March 14, 1975, when thirteen-year old Dana Bonafacio was raped and shot to death at Kiona'ole Road near the Pali Golf Course. Bonafacio and her friend, Cheryl Vera Cruz, were kidnapped from a bus stop in Kailua at gunpoint and forced into a vehicle. Vera Cruz managed to escape at the scene of the crime.

Dewey Eddondons, a former Marine stationed at Kane'ohe, is presently in custody after being extradited from Indiana, his home state. He will be tried for the alleged kidnapping and murder. He will also, we are told, undergo DNA testing as well. Dana Bonafacio would have been 39 years old today had she lived...."

And they flashed her picture on the screen. This time I did drop the iron, scalding the floor. The mark is still there, an omen or a reminder of some sort, and I have to explain to my wife why I don't have it removed. Come to think of it, I have to explain it to myself. I never met Dana Bonafacio that Friday night on the bus, but other people had seen her. I met her a few days after the tour, on a TV screen; we were introduced by a businesslike newscaster in a power suit. Her hair is reddish-brown, and she's hapa, and she wears granny glasses from the Seventies. In college we used to study something called the collective unconscious, and it made for great bull sessions. But all this just makes me freeze with fear and sadness.

▼ ▼ ▼

Tolentino called that night, agitated. I calmed him down a bit. "Boss," he began to say.

"My name's not Boss," I said to him. "I'm your friend."

"Boss," he said. "The girl. I saw the news. I neva' say nothing on the bus, but I seen her. I tell you, I seen her when I stopped da bus. I put my head down on da wheel, I pray, I look up, she standing right in front me. I see her on TV tonight. You gotta do something, boss, She need help. And I gotta tell you, I cannot drive. I called the company, I quit already. Thanks boss, you one good guy. Take care."

Like I said, you've gotta go along with me on this one, cut me some slack. I get sad every time I think about it, there's a spot the shape of an iron on the kitchen floor that's going to stay there, and I think Tolentino and a lot of other people understand the fluidity of time and memory better than I do.

Long Ago and
Oh So Far Away

Every now and then, I have a horrible nightmare. In it, there are two thirteen-year-old girls—Dana and Cheryl are their names—waiting for a bus in Kailua. Cheryl is dark-haired, with a fair complexion. Dana has auburn hair, and in the light of the sun, streaks of blonde. They are young, vibrant and happy, with the entire world waiting for them. Their future has not yet been carved in stone.

They are singing—a Karen Carpenter tune from the Seventies—"Every sha la la la, every whoa, oh oh still shines...every shinga linga ling that they're startin' to sing, so fine...."

Then a blue Plymouth Dart, blue, the color of a robin's egg, pulls up with four guys inside. The driver's name is Dewey Eddendons. He's a square-jawed Marine, full of testosterone and ready to prove it. The faces of the other men are hazy and unfocused, but they all seem to know each other. It looks as though Dana and Cheryl know them too. The back door of the car opens, and as the girls climb into the back seat, I am filled with paralyzing dread. They sit on the laps of the guys in the back. I watch helplessly as Dana and Cheryl recede through the rear windshield, mouthing the word "bye" in unison.

I'm standing at an angle where I can see Dewey and we lock eyes. He smiles at me. It is a cold, sadistic smile, a Cheshire cat grin with the promise of violence in it. I see him reach over to the glove compartment. He pulls out a pistol and points it right at me.

Bang!

Bang! Bang! Bang!

And before I feel anything, I wake up in a cold sweat, gasping for breath.

▼　▼　▼

It's a hell of a dream. I'd dozed off one afternoon and it was starting again; my wife and daughter were out shopping for the day. I was awakened by a loud knock, and I remember wondering who would be knocking on my door this early in the morning. Then I woke suddenly, saw my clock, and realized that it was three in the afternoon.

I opened the front door. It took me a minute, but I recognized him as Eric, the psychic I'd taken on a tour—the one who'd pulled me aside at Morgan's

Corner and made an unnerving prediction. I liked the guy, but my first reaction was one of irritation.

"How do you know where I live?" I asked.

"Do I really have to explain?" Eric asked, and I had to smile at that. I let him in. "What's up?" I asked. "You seem bothered."

He looked at me for a long time. When a psychic does that, it kind of makes you squirm inside. "Look," he said finally. "I'm gonna just come out and say it. I know—I'm certain that there was more than one person involved in that girl Dana's murder. Maybe Dewey shot her, but there were others involved. Probably three others."

I gasped, and began rocking back and forth on the balls of my feet. I shook my head, muttering to myself, "It's yesterday once more."

"Say what?" asked Eric.

"Nothing." I waved him off. "I was just talking to myself."

"No really. What did you say?"

"I said 'It's yesterday once more.'"

"Damn," he said, and I think his voice quivered a bit. "I had a vision, and I saw the whole murder. It didn't happen the way the news reported it. *Yesterday Once More.*" He shook his head. "Karen Carpenter. The song played over and over in my head during the vision, and I couldn't place it until now. Damn. Where'd you hear it?"

"In a dream I keep having," I said. "About Dana."

The silence in the room was deafening.

▼ ▼ ▼

My day began with a knock on the door at three in the afternoon, and wouldn't end until three the next morning. I made a note to myself to ditch all my Carpenters tapes and discs.

Close to You

I hadn't seen or heard from Eric in quite some time. One night, I led a blissfully uneventful tour which ended at Morgan's Corner. I remember feeling somewhat relieved that he hadn't come along. Don't get me wrong; I liked the guy—sort of. But I'm a spiritual explorer and tour guide, and Eric had already been there, and his terse and often smug predictions had made me uneasy for months.

I said "blissfully uneventful." The world that I explore is a remarkable one, a gift, perhaps giving me some wisdom beyond the ordinary. But it's also a heavy burden sometimes, and one hell of a responsibility. I've mentioned my caution in opening spiritual doors, and this is because they never really close again. They can be dangerous, not only for me but for the people I try to teach.

Through the entire tour that night, I remember thinking that the ghosts and spirits and I were simply taking a day off. As we stopped at different locations, some people were frightened, but only in the way normal people get when they visit haunted places. There was not a peep, or a vision, or a sign of anything otherwordly at all.

A day off, I thought. And as the minibus hummed down the highway toward home, I fell asleep immediately. And then I dreamed.

It was a Morgan's Corner dream, ominous and familiar. The pavement on the road was new, brand new. The branches from the trees that arch over the road now were not there. And even the haunted tree—the hugging tree—seemed to harbor no menace; it seemed lighter, even carefree.

I was at Morgan's Corner, but I wasn't really there at all. It was a still Ko'olau day. And then the silence was broken, rudely and violently, by gunshots. They were the same gunshots I'd heard in the dream when Dewey Eddendons pointed his handgun at me and fired.

I heard screaming from somewhere up the road, and heard five more shots. I had no concern for my own safety, and I walked toward the sound of the gunfire. I found myself at the top of Kiona'ole Road, and saw Dewey and his three friends run right past me, furiously. As in my previous dream, I couldn't identify his friends. But Dewey stopped, looked me dead in the eye, and flipped me the bird. I did notice that all of them were covered with blood.

Then I heard tires screeching, the noise disappearing in the air. As if in a trance—a dream within a dream—I walked mechanically and involuntarily back down the road. I knew all the time what I would find, and I did. Just off the side of the pavement lay Dana's crumpled body. I saw her once radiant, beautiful hair matted with her own blood, and then I couldn't look anymore. Turning away, I ran into a woman and drew in my breath.

She didn't react at all. She was staring at Dana with tired eyes, full of sadness and deep weariness. She was crying, too, and it seemed to me somehow that she had shed the same tears many times before.

And then I realized that the woman was Cheryl. She was thirty-odd years older, but there was no mistaking her.

Finally she spoke, her voice cracking, nearly devoid of feeling. "I didn't do anything. I didn't do anything." She sounded resigned, her emotional well tapped dry.

"Of course you didn't do anything," I blurted. "Dewey did this."

She looked at me, her head shaking very slowly. "No," she said, "I ran away.

"I ran away," she repeated. "If I'd just have stayed, this wouldn't have..." Her gaze was both blank and imploring. "If I had stayed. It was just sex, after all. That's all they wanted. What difference would that have made? But Dewey and his friends wanted to do it—you know—all at the same time. And I wasn't ready, so I panicked and I ran. I ran so fast...if I had just stayed and done what they wanted, Dana would still be alive."

I had been watching her closely, and her face was full of tired regret and heartbreak. Then it changed into terror, and I knew someone was behind me. I spun around and found myself face-to-face with Dewey. His gun was pointed at my head, its hammer cocked back. I screamed "Nooooooooo" like they do in movies where someone keeps falling and falling and then disappears. And he pulled the trigger.

I bolted upright, fully awake and sweaty. The bus had stopped, letting the last passengers out. I started breathing deeply to regain some semblance of composure. The driver was half-standing, half-sitting in his seat, looking at me curiously. "Brah, you OK or what?"

"Yeah, I'm OK," I muttered. "Thanks." Then I got off the bus and walked a ways. Maybe, I thought, I wasn't getting enough sleep. Or maybe I'd just gotten myself too involved with Dana and the murder. And I silently cursed Eric and his damned predictions.

For a couple of months after that, I didn't do any tours. For one thing, I had a book to write. For another, I needed to get away from the dilemma.

And one day, I was taking a long overdue shower when the phone rang. I got out, soaking wet, and answered it, and heard Eric at the other end. No hellos, no how-you-beens. "Dude," he barked, "turn on the TV. Now!"

I hate taking orders, but there was something about Eric.... I moved toward the TV, phone in hand, and said, "You're about a year too late, aren't you?"

"Yeah, yeah," Eric said impatiently. "I know. Just turn it on and watch the news." I did, right in the middle of a report:

"...DNA samples did not match. Eddendons was released after nearly a year in custody. He said he was happy that he'd been found innocent, and wants to go back home to live his life."

There was a commercial, and I turned off the TV in anger. Eric was still on the line. "Damn!" I said. "After all that, the bastard goes scot-free." I knew Eric was still there; I could hear him breathing. I could almost hear him thinking.

"That night," he said, "I was supposed to come with you on a tour and channel Dana's ghost—you know, at Morgan's Corner? Well...she didn't come there. She came to me."

It was my turn to take a deep breath. "What in the hell are you talking about?" I asked coldly.

"I mean," said Eric, his voice precise, schoolmasterish, prim—"that as I was about to leave my house, she sat on my shoulders, like a kid playing horsy. And then, she took over my body.

"She took over my body, that's right. Then she took over my mind, and I knew everything she knew. You know why the DNA samples didn't match? Because there were other people involved besides Dewey.

"You told me about your dreams," he continued, and he sounded a bit dreamy himself. "I had more than a dream. I felt everything—the rape, the beating, the shooting, the blood, the thud of being thrown on the side of the road like trash. And I could feel the life leaving her body, her last thought being that she did not want to die this way, alone, away from her parents and her sister.

"This whole thing," and Eric's speech had slowed down to a crawl—"this thing messed me up pretty bad, 'cause it kept happening, over and over again. I tried moving several times, but each time, she found me. It made me want to believe in something, so I became a minister—ordained. But I bit off more than I could chew. I couldn't preach, and I couldn't comfort anyone."

I was speechless. Eric was speaking almost normally now, but there was an electricity in his voice that had nothing to do with the phone line.

"I gotta hang up now, but I have to tell you one more thing. I saw you standing over me, or Dana—believe it if you want, or don't—and I saw you talking to Cheryl. I saw Dewey fire the gun." He paused for a bit. "You died." The phone went *click* and I backed into my armchair, still clad in a towel. For a moment, I wondered who was the bigger son-of-a-bitch—Dewey or Eric.

There are questions you want answered, and others you'd rather not. It was all physically impossible anyway. I did check the caller ID on my phone. It read *Hawai'i State Hospital*, and, for a while, everything made a bit of sense.

But every now and then I wonder about what happens to overworked minds. I think about time, about being stuck in 1975, the year Dana was killed, and wonder why she didn't take hold of me as well.

And I think about Eric. Maybe he'd been a patient all along; maybe I'd met him on a weekend pass. I'll never know. And as time goes by, I think about him less and less.

Not long ago, I took another group to Morgan's Corner for the usual stories and tree-huggings, and we turned back toward the bus. For some reason, I looked back at the haunted tree, so innocent in my dreams and so mature with meaning and menace now. And I saw Dana, as plainly as though it were daylight. She smiled ever so slightly at me.

I began sobbing uncontrollably. Fortunately, I was some distance from everyone and it was pitch dark out.

Later that night, at home, I sat on the edge of the bed and watched my wife and daughter sleep. And I realized how profoundly and deeply I loved them, and silently thanked the powers that be for my great fortune. For somewhere in the past—or future—who knows?—it is always 1975. And there is a lonely stretch of road near a hairpin turn where there will always be a fourteen-year-old girl whose gruesome death became a legend—the legend of Morgan's Corner.

The Tree and the Toe

I love my job, and the groups are generally a joy to lead. But occasionally, a drunk or two will join us. More often than not, they fall asleep on the bus, causing little bother. Occasionally, they are loud and boorish, and I have to ask them either to behave or leave.

Once a couple joined the group on an investigation. We didn't know it at the time, but she was loaded. She hid it well—as well as she hid the flask of apricot brandy in her purse.

She wasn't loud or obnoxious, but she was antisocial. Whenever we got off the bus, she'd stand about ten feet away from the group. She did it at Morgan's Corner. While everyone else hugged the haunted tree, half-hoping to see the restless spirits that inhabit its branches, she was at first silent. Then, out of the blue, she screamed at the top of her lungs. "Ahhhhh! Aaahhhh! Somebody stepped on my toe! My toe! I goin' sue you guys for liability!" Everyone pretended to ignore her, even her husband.

When we got back to the bus, the husband could take no more. He really lit into her. "What the hell you talking about?" he snapped. "You were at least ten feet away from the group, like you always are. Nobody came near you, and nobody stepped on your toe. So shut up already!"

That stopped her cold, and suddenly we could all smell the alcohol on her breath. This infuriated her husband. "Drinking again? See? You see? You imagining things! Stepped on your toe, my foot."

"Besides," he said, "who told you to wear slippers?"

With that, she looked down at her foot. It was dark, and she grabbed the flashlight out of my hand, shining it directly on her right foot. She gasped. The nail on the big toe was gone, revealing flesh and blood. Ripped clean.

She handed me the flashlight and stepped on the bus with as much dignity as she could retrieve. She said nothing the rest of the night.

▼ ▼ ▼

The next day, her husband called me. She'd explained everything to him. She'd walked ahead of us because she had to make *shishi* very badly. At the first tree she could find, she squatted, urinating on the bottom of the trunk, finishing in time to wait for us as though nothing had happened.

But the tree was the legendary one, the haunted tree that houses the restless spirits of the dead. I heard that when she found that out, she went cold turkey and gave up the bottle. But you never know for sure about these things.

The Jackass

He appears from time to time in all of my investigations. He's usually a young guy, who lets it be known that he would really rather be home watching a game on TV. He has an air of studied indifference and an abrasive ego to match. With an air of resignation, he is able to imply that his wife or girlfriend is downright foolish for venturing out at night in search of spirits. I call this guy the Jackass—a nice generic name—and I do my best to ignore him. Most of the time, he is simply irritates others, but every now and then, he creates trouble for himself. It's rather uncharitable of me, but when he does, I feel a certain quiet satisfaction. But that's beside the point.

Once we had a seventeen-year-old boy along on tour with his girlfriend. His manners, even by the standards of a Jackass, were rude to the point of caricature. He'd interrupt our investigation with questions that had nothing to do with anything. Then he'd make some feeble attempt to frighten other people in the group, which would do nothing more than get on their nerves. His girlfriend tried to simmer him down, but gave up.

The guy was a pain in the ass. We took a break at McDonald's, and he decided to hide in the womens' bathroom, frightening them as they entered. At that point, I had to pull him aside, and as politely as I could, through gritted teeth, tell him to control himself. Otherwise, I said, I would leave him behind with his girlfriend, and he could spend the weekend explaining that away to her. That seemed to work. He looked at least half contrite, and promised to behave.

And, indeed, everything went just fine, until we reached our last stop at Morgan's Corner. Now Morgan's Corner is a magical place, mysterious beyond comprehension, its trees tall and overwhelming and, some say, haunted. There is only one way to tell if a tree is haunted, and that is to hug it and look at its branches. If someone does see the dark and restless spirits that haunt the tree, and the spirits see them, they're stuck to the tree, unable to free themselves.

Naturally, the Jackass was the first to hug the tree. Actually, he didn't hug it. He mounted it. He jumped up on the trunk of the tree and began to move his hips like a rock singer, singing, in a scratchy falsetto, "Oooooh, yeah, baby! Yeeeah tree! Uh! Uh!"

I turned away, not knowing whether to laugh or spit in disgust. His girlfriend was embarrassed. All the others simply ignored him, and took turns hugging the same tree. They did so quietly and reverently, with just a trace of fear.

When it was time to leave, we did a quick head count, and the Jackass was missing. We asked his girlfriend, and she swore he was right behind her. Swearing to myself, I went back up the road to find him, and the group started to follow me. Every one of them will vouch for what we saw next.

He was squatting next to the tree, his head down, crying. His girlfriend knelt down next to him, and the next thing we heard was her scream. "Oh, my God!" she said over and over.

She looked up at us in helpless fear, and her words were measured and drawn out, the way some people talk when frightened. "There is someone sitting on his shoulders. On his shoulders! I put my hand on the back of his neck and I felt someone's thighs. But I can't see anybody!" She wept openly now, shaking, and a guy in the group put his arm around her to comfort her. Others were praying, and I heard a voice asking if he should call 911.

I went up to him, and it suddenly seemed to me that the tree was larger than I remembered. "Brother," I asked him, "what's happening? You OK?" He was still crying, and he reminded me of a scared little kid who'd just been bitten by a vicious dog. He looked up at me, his eyes red and his face swollen.

"I can't stand up. There's somebody sitting on my shoulders and I can't get up. Please, please, I'm sorry! I'm sorry, I really am!"

To tell the truth, I had no sympathy for him, but I asked, in my best professional manner, "When did it happen?" I knew the answer.

"When I was done hugging the tree," he sobbed, "I felt it grab me by the shoulders and it jumped on me. It's really strong, mister. It won't let me go and it keeps laughing at me. Make it stop!"

I drew in my breath. "Kid," I said, "if this is another one of your lame tricks, I swear, I'm going to leave you here all alone, and never think about you again. That's a promise."

"Not!" he screamed. "Not, I promise! Feel my shoulders!"

I did. There was nothing there, but his whole body was hot—so hot you could feel it before touching him.

I said, "OK, brother, it's up to you. You gotta apologize. Not to me. To them—those spirits above you in the tree. Maybe, just maybe, they'll forgive you."

He looked up slowly and pleaded, apologizing so profusely I thought that even the spirits might be a bit embarrassed. But after a minute or so, he could stand a bit, and walked, hunched over, toward the bus. One of the group members was an old Hawaiian lady, and as he passed her she said, "Good for you! We shoulda thrown you off the Pali when we had the chance."

The ride back to town was unusually quiet. Everyone took care to thank me, even the Jackass. He looked so miserable I nearly felt sorry for him. But then I realized that there were lots more like him, and didn't think about him at all any more.

Why Do They Do That?

I've spoken often about Morgan's Corner—its mystery, its beauty and its terror. It is full of restless spirits, particularly those of those who have met their ends there. I once compared it to a cathedral, and it must be approached with at least as much respect and awe.

Having said that, it is as beautiful and scenic a place to hike as one could find anywhere. There is ginger, both white and yellow, growing wild. Hau wood grows in wild abundance—perfect for cutting to fashion kala'au—dancing sticks—for a hula class. And the other large trees are breathtaking.

But the one thing I've noticed—or not noticed—during the day is the sound of birds. There are no birds, and this makes the atmosphere a bit too still and quiet, to the point of becoming unnerving. And at night, Morgan's Corner changes with a sudden force that chills the blood.

All in all—and I've sung its praises often enough—Morgan's Corner can be a very dark place, a haven for evil. For one thing, it's a dumping ground for appliances, old cars, and the proverbial kitchen sink. And—on occasion—human bodies.

First of all, Morgan's Corner is approached on an isolated stretch of road with no street lights. It's frightening beyond belief for anyone who stumbles across it by accident.

It has hairpin turns, and a joyride can be fatal. In 1989, a young woman was thrown from the back of a truck and killed during a drag race. And there have been some brutal murders committed there. For all of its beauty, Morgan's Corner has a lot of negative energy—a beautiful garden peppered with deadly weeds.

And in spite of this, or because of it, it attracts certain people who go there at night to tempt those forces. Perhaps they want to capture them on camera, or scare a girlfriend the way one might do at a horror movie. Wiccans—pagans who believe in the power of earth and spirits—sometimes go there as apprentices, wishing to channel a wandering ghost, and end up channeling far more than they bargained for.

Perhaps, I often reflect, it's the sort of place that attracts the people we call adrenaline junkies. And perhaps they are no more mad than, say, race car drivers or skydivers. It's a cliche, but it's also true—it takes all kinds.

That's not why I go there. I tell ghost stories and lead guided tours, and take a daring few to Morgan's Corner. But there is a line I will not cross—not for my sake, but for the sake of the people who have trusted me as a teacher and a guide.

Most of them know little about the rules and protocols of dealing with ghosts, spirits and other supernatural phenomenon. I have to use my best judgment. For me to lift the veil which separates our world from the world of the dead could well prove harmful, opening doors that can never again be closed. My job, as I see it, is that of a teacher and student, providing a moving seminar on the Hawaiian spiritual tradition that has shaped my own life so profoundly. To do less—to provide cheap thrills—would be a betrayal. I would no longer be a storyteller; instead I would be a seedy used-car salesman. And death would be my customer.

Here, then, are a few accounts—cautionary tales, really—of people who have crossed that invisible line for foolish and shortsighted purposes—and who have paid for it one way or another. There is no other way to describe their actions except in terms of folly, plain and simple. I don't preach—I tell stories. But unlike Erasmus, I do not praise folly. I want to warn everyone—myself included—to avoid it.

No Security

As I've said, I make a living leading groups who explore the supernatural, and most of the people in them are courteous, well-mannered, and curious. And so are the people we meet along the way. Once in a while, though, I run into a real horse's ass—someone with no connection whatsoever to our work who decides to act like a fool. My policy is simple. I tell them to go away. It usually works. Once it didn't. The jerk in question was wearing a uniform. I also have a policy of never bothering anyone in uniform.

This is a strange story, which may be filled to the brim with meaning, or it may have none whatsoever. I still don't know. It happened recently, in March of this year, while I was guiding a group through 'Iolani Palace. There had been reports that the ghost of Queen Kapi'olani had appeared a few times near the banyan tree in the back of the Palace, and others that she had been seen outside the back porch of the throne room.

It was early evening when we pulled up, and there was a white moped parked near one of the banyans. As we got out, we heard the sound of a two-way radio—the kind the cops use—coming right from the moped. It was a crackle, nothing more, and I figured it belonged to a security guard.

Then we heard another buzz and crackle, followed by a voice, like someone imitating a ghost—"Ooooooooooooo! Ooooooooooooo!" Jeez, I thought to myself. What's the world coming to when a security guard has nothing better to do than try and scare a busload of strangers?

For some reason, I glanced up at one of the shutters. There was a guard, who threw them open, pressing his face against the window in a grotesque caricature.

I didn't say anything, but I remember figuring the guy was going to get fired, and I had a sour feeling inside that told me that the world was full of jerks. We proceeded with our investigation and went home.

About a week later, we were back at the palace, and were joined by a few docents—volunteers who conduct tours through the Palace. In a fit of pique, I mentioned the guard to them. As I finished the story, I saw that they were looking at me curiously, some frowning, some bewildered.

Finally, one of them placed his hand on my arm gently and said, "We have a security system. There are no guards here at night." He looked at me with a sad smile on his face, as if to say you've really been taking this business too seriously.

Maybe I was, and maybe I still do. I really don't know. Something tells me I never will.

Thhpptt

It's an odd title, but a true story. During any investigation there are a certain number of cynics and nonbelievers—as opposed to the merely skeptical—and I treat them like everyone else. All I ask is that they keep their opinions to themselves or stay home, so that those who are interested and those who truly believe are not disturbed.

Not too long ago I led a group to several sites, and every time I finished telling a story—one inevitably dealing with ghosts, hauntings, and the supernatural—a young girl standing in the back of the group would make a noise. It's a noise known as the Bronx cheer or the raspberry on the Mainland, and it's nearly impossible to reproduce on paper:

"Thhpptt!"

She kept doing it everywhere we went, every time I'd finish my story. She showed no embarrassment over it. We went to a Japanese cemetery. I told a story.

"Thhpptt!"

We proceeded to a shopping mall where there'd been some reported hauntings.

"Thhpptt!"

We went to the bridge on 16th Avenue, reportedly haunted, and I told the story in great detail.

"Thhpptt!"

We went to a Chinese cemetery.

"Thhpptt!"

Finally, we went to the Pali lookout. After I finished talking, I heard another "Thhpptt!" My patience and humor had diminished greatly as the evening wore on.

"That's it!" I yelled at her. I walked over to her, figuring a silent stare was better than any lecture at this point. But the girl seemed genuinely shocked. I had to say something after all. In a sardonic voice, I asked, "Have I done something wrong? Did I offend you this evening in some way?"

She was open-mouthed with surprise. "No—no, not at all. Why do you ask?"

"Because," I hissed through my teeth, "You keep making that damned noise all night. Everywhere we go. Every time I speak."

Her contrition seemed genuine enough, and she hung her head in abject apology, and I began to believe her. But I kept my arms folded and my eyes fixed on her.

"I'm—I'm so sorry! I'm—well, I'm just so scared that I need to do something. You know, to reassure myself that none of this is real."

I was calmer now, but was still tired of it all; the same joke over and over can get on your nerves. "Please," I said to her, "stop it. It's irritating."

▼　▼　▼

We then boarded the bus and headed for Morgan's Corner. As you know by now, it's a complicated place, and I explained what to do and what not to do very clearly. The ritual there, of course, is the hugging of the haunted tree. Everyone took turns, some eagerly, some reluctantly. When the girl went up to hug the tree, something very odd happened. As soon as she touched it, she began to fart uncontrollably. Can you guess what sound it was that came out of her? Thhpptts! We all had to hold our mouths and noses to keep from laughing out loud.

Myself, I've never quite figured out what happened, or why. But it's a true story.

The Black Hand

Mario wasn't built at all like a Filipino, save for his height, which was about five feet, four inches. He had no neck, a barrel chest, a muscular torso, and arms like Popeye. His calves were shaped like huge diamonds. He belonged to a karate school called The Black Hand. They practiced *kempo*.

In its heyday—the Seventies and the Eighties—The Black Hand was one of the toughest *dojos* in town. Its members always got top honors in tournaments. But in the Nineties they suddenly went underground, nearly impossible to find. This added a bit of mystery and intrigue to my friendship with Mario.

One night, Mario and I were talking story at a Pizza Hut in Waipahu—stories about this and that, and nothing in particular. Then, suddenly, his voice became a low whisper. "Can we talk outside?"

I looked around. "Sure," I said. And we went to the parking lot, standing by his truck.

Even in the dark, I could see that he was looking intently at me. "You know I belong to the Black Hand, right?"

"Sure," I said. "How could I not know? You keep reminding me."

The humor was lost on him. "I told you we practice *kempo*, right?" His voice was edgier, almost like a physical push.

I was apprehensive, but stood my ground. "Yeah."

"Well," he said, "That's what we want people to think. What we're actually doing is practicing lua."

That got my attention. "You mean—you mean the Hawaiian martial art? That kind of lua?" He nodded, and I felt a knot in my stomach. Lua is hand-to-hand combat, dangerous and often deadly.

After a long silence, I said, very slowly, "Mario, lua isn't something you sign up for and quit. It's a way of life. It's not a nine-to-five thing you do during the week and put on the shelf for the weekend. Mario, it's all or nothing. My father once told me that lua often involves sorcery. You understand that?"

I said that to sober him, but he became arrogant. "Of course I know that! Who's practicing it, anyway, you or me? I gotta get an OK from you?" I had never seen him this angry before. "Look," I said, "just calm down and relax, OK?"

And this backfired; it only made him angrier. "*You* calm down!" He was screaming now. I was on the verge of screaming back, and then realized I was suddenly talking to a stranger. I spun around, got into my own car, and drove off. My tires squealed. I don't normally do that.

After that, Mario disappeared for a while; no one knew his whereabouts. Maybe a year later, I was involved in producing a play at a community college, and I saw Mario backstage. At first I didn't recognize him; he was lighter and trimmer now, and he was, of all things, smiling.

He came up to me. "Lopaka, my brother!" He gave me a suffocating hug. "How you been?"

"Great, great!" I replied, happy to see him, and surprised."And you?"

He sighed. "Man, I'm really sorry about that time last year. All I can tell you is that it was the worst time of my life. I was fighting with my parents every day, and my girlfriend wasn't speaking to me. My fault, man. I was being mean and cruel to her—even calling her names...." His voice drifted off. "And all that was the time I was with the Black Hand."

"No sweat, Mario," I said.

"Yeah, thanks. But that's why I got so mad at you that night—you remember? Because you were right. We were practicing lua all right, but not the lua that everybody knows. We were doing the sorcery too."

"Man! Mario!" I said, and my own skin was crawling, even though I didn't know what kind of sorcery they were involved with.

"There was this old banyan tree," said Mario, "right in the middle of a park in Kapolei. Five of us would surround it and hit the trunk with our open palms. And you know what? The bark would tear off, and the whole tree would shake." Mario twisted his body, trying to emulate a horse. He thrust both hands out in front of him, palms open, and yelled, "HEEEEEEEE!" The sound vibrated and went right through me.

"Man, I was so full of myself back then. Anyway, one night afterwards, I got home about two in the morning. I kept thinking to myself how I couldn't wait to get out of the damn house—away from my parents, and even my girlfriend. Well, all the lights in the house were off. Dad was snoring. Mom was asleep. My room was in the back of the house. When I got there, I opened the door and reached for the light. No windows in my room—it was pitch black. So anyway, I reach for the light switch, and suddenly I get grabbed by the wrist and tossed completely across the room. Hit the wall hard; saw stars. I heard my bedroom door slam at the same time. I remember thinking some thief had broken into the house, and I surprised him. Now I could use my lua—in self-defense.

"Well, I thought I could, anyhow. Whoever this guy was, he was quicker and stronger than me. Every time he hit me, I reached out for his arm so I could get him in a lua hold and break him in two. But he was always just out of reach, and he kept hitting me. I then turned chicken, and I yelled at him to be still—ridiculous, yeah? But that's when I heard the deepest, most evil laugh I've ever heard in my life. My spine went cold.

"I knew then he was toying with me, and I realized he'd kill me any second. And without warning, I was picked up and thrown down onto my bed, and the guy was on me. He was choking me now, and the world started to spin. I made one last grab for his arms, but there was nothing there. Nothing at all. Nothing had me pinned to my bed, and I remember thinking this is a ridiculous way to die. Choked to death by a ghost.

"Then, suddenly, it let go, and it was gone."

His voice was dreamy but clear. "I cried, for the first time since I was a kid. I woke up early in the morning, and I walked slowly to the breakfast table. It took a while, but I hugged both my parents, which caught them off-guard, and I begged their forgiveness. And they gave it to me.

"Then I went to my girlfriend's house to ask her for mercy. This was not so easy, and it took some time to heal. In the meantime, I got a job. Security guard. Kūlanakauhale Resort.

"Great job; I loved it. Or I did, until one night I got a call from some guests on the fourteenth floor. They'd heard some commotion, and someone had been throwing things around in the room. Other guests could hear furniture breaking, glass shattering. So I looked for the room, and it was 1403.

"Remember my address—91-1403 Helepololei Street? 1403. Blew my mind, man."

Mario paused for a bit. I said nothing. "Anyway, I swiped the key card into the door and it opened. The room was dark, and all the lights were off. Guess what happened? Same thing! Guy grabs me, pins me down, I feel his teeth on my knuckles, and then the guy gets me in a headlock. This time it's a real person; that much I know. He had a vise grip on my neck, but I managed to grab his forearm—it felt like a steel cable—and I pushed, hard as I could. I was free. I ran to the door and turned the light on. I had to see his face.

"I turned the light on. The room was immaculate. Nothing broken. No one there. So what I did was I quit, that night. I work somewhere now where no ghosts try to harass me."

"Where?" I asked.

"Hālawa Prison," he said.

Theater Number 6

Back in July of '02, I met a woman who had managed a movie theater. She told me that she had a hard time keeping employees; they would quit after less than a month on the job. She was a talker, I tell you. I liked her.

"Two weeks ago," she told me, "I hired a 73-year-old Filipino man—retired, but he needed something to do. I gave him the shift between two in the afternoon to ten at night. He was great. Despite his age, he worked hard and never complained.

"One day, another worker called in sick, leaving no one to cover the closing shift. I asked the old man if he could stay a bit longer. He said no problem, so long as someone could take him home, since the bus stopped running at 10:30 pm.

"I gave him theater number 6 to clean that night after the last show, and the entire shift went by without incident. A little after midnight, I was in the lobby chewing out two young employees for goofing off on duty. Out of the corner of my eye, I saw the old man entering theater 6 with a broom and a garbage bin.

"And suddenly, we heard a scream, the kind you hear in the horror movies when the sound is up. We saw him run out of the theater, and the look on his face is one I'll never forget. He looked like he'd seen Death.

"We chased after him, of course, but he was fast. He ran up a flight of stairs and across a parking lot, jumped over a fence, and ran past a service station, and even cut across the freeway. He finally stopped at a church.

"I caught up with him—those two young good-for-nothings with me gave up back at the parking lot—and I found him kneeling in front of the church praying, with a rosary in his hands.

"I put my hand on his shoulder—he was shaking—and I said the strangest thing—I guess it was my way of trying to make things normal again. I said 'I hate to tell you this, papa, but you gotta finish your shift!'

"He turned his head around, still clutching the rosary, and said quietly, 'OK, boss. But somebody else gotta clean that theater. Otherwise pau'—and he moved his right hand in an arc, like a sideways karate chop—'and I quit!'

"I had to agree, and I walked him back real slow to the theater with my arm around him. I figured I could do it while he stood outside, and he was his old self by the time we got back. So I went in—the broom and the bin were still there—and I started picking up popcorn cups, and sodas, and napkins.

"In the middle of the theater there's a row of seats reserved for people in wheelchairs. I'd almost filled the bin and was reaching for the broom when I saw a woman—a ragged woman, maybe homeless—sitting in the very last seat in that row. Now this sort of thing happens often, and usually I just ask the person to go—real gentle-like, you know? So I went over, tapped her on the shoulder, and as I did, I felt a cold chill. The woman looked up at me, and I saw her tattered clothing. Her hair was long, white, wet and matted.

"She stood bolt upright and looked right at me, and I felt like running myself. Her white hair was hanging over her face. I was transfixed, as though I had been glued to the floor, unable to speak or move. And the chill! Nothing like it before or since." Her laugh was quick and nervous.

"She started to reach forward and she grabbed her own hair, pulling it away. You won't believe this. There was no face. Just an—an—ahh what do you call it—an orb of flesh, no features at all.

"And that's all I remember. I fainted. Somebody found me in the middle of the theater about three in the morning, and they took me home. I didn't dare tell them anything. They would have driven me straight to the psych ward.

"It took me two days to recover. I ain't working at that theater ever again, although I think the old man is still there, and I hear he's happy as he can be and whistles all the time.You know anyone who wants to manage a theater?"

A Ghost at the Cleaners

I follow all kinds of rumors for a living. Most people associate hauntings with exotic, strange and obscure locations. True believers, though, will often find them in supermarkets or a dry cleaners.

The summer of '02 was hot—the kind of hot that slows the pulse and makes the whole world turn sluggish. Futless, we say in Hawai'i. But I had heard that the ghost of a faceless woman had been seen in a supermarket, wandering up and down the aisles during the day, in the middle of crowds. I was skeptical, but I took a group there anyway, and was only mildly encouraged when a guy in back of the group told me that he was a clerk at the market and had seen the haunting. Big deal, I thought to myself, but I nodded at him anyway.

"The funniest part about it is this, though," he continued. "The store was already haunted."

Now I was interested. "Tell me some more," I said.

"Well," said the guy, a bit shy but pleased at suddenly being the center of attention, "the employee bathroom is haunted. It's the maintenance man."

"You know that for sure?" I asked.

"Yeah, for sure," he said. "He was repairing a light fixture in the bathroom. Then he had to use the can, and when he sat on it, he died of a heart attack. He's been haunting the bathroom ever since."

I thought about that one for a while, and wondered if he was putting me on. So I looked at the group with a poker face. "Just think about that," I said. "You wake up in the morning. You use the toilet, and you never get off of it alive. Instead, you end up haunting it."

The laughter was subdued and nervous. It ended suddenly as the group jumped back, almost in unison, with their eyes staring beyond me. I turned around, and, involuntarily, I jumped back as well. In fact, I think I screamed, a bit too loudly.

I was face-to-face with the manager of the dry cleaners, which was next door to the supermarket. She was short, maybe five feet tall, with the kind of beehive hairdo you see on old country-western singers. It was dyed jet black. The rest of her hair was very long, and it fell down her back to her knees. She was too tan, and I was reminded momentarily of a fried malasada. Her eyebrows were thin and penciled in over huge doe-like eyes with way too much eyeliner. I'll never forget her.

Her voice was something else, shrill and high and abrasive—a caricature of a tita.

"Eh! I know you, brah! You da one coming ovah heah telling ghos' stories. Right in front my store! I tell you now. Get out, no come back! You come back, I have you arrested! If that no work, I get friends!"

This business is odd enough without getting arrested or worse, so I started to back off, and I put my hands up as a peace gesture. "OK," I said, "But tell me why."

"Why?" Her eyes bore holes into me. "Because evah since you been coming around telling ghos' stories—da faceless lady, or whatevah—she haunting my place now. My business! You understand! Now get outta heah!"

I think the blood had drained from my face, and my shriek had not done much for my credibility as a leader. So I turned very carefully to the group, looking over their heads to avoid direct eye contact. "We better get back on the bus," I said. Everyone quietly followed me.

But before we could board the bus, I noticed two young guys who had come out of the side exit of the cleaner's. They seemed eager, and didn't seem to want trouble. They came up to me and whispered, "Look, brah, we gotta tell you something." They looked like brothers. I motioned to the group. There was one big guy in the bunch who would keep an eye on me just in case.

"You guys brothers?" I asked, just to break the ice. They nodded. They led me to the front of a gas station next door. One of them said, "I heard everything, and I gotta tell you...." and he paused for a bit, swallowing deeply. "My name Darrell. This my kid brother, Jason. We heard, just now, and we like...we like tell you...we know."

"We know," Jason repeated. His voice sounded like a chant. " Last week Tuesday, my brother and me was closing up the store like always, and we was headed toward our car. We heard some kind of pounding sound, so we turned around, and we saw this short girl—black shorts, blue tank top. And she's bent over with her head aimed at the store. And...."

Darrell cut in. "And she took two steps back and was ramming her head into the side exit door. That's our store, you know."

Jason said, "Yeah, same door we just came out of. I tell you, full on, brah! She was ramming her head into that door and shaking it. We was afraid the door was goin' broke!"

I whistled. "So what did you guys do?"

Darrell was animated now. "I told my brother to go see if she was OK. Then, for some reason, I ran to the car to get crackers and poi. Don't ask me why."

He laughed nervously. "We always get crackers and poi in the car. I dunno why."

"And while he was doing that," said Jason, "I ran up right next to her and I was begging and yelling for her to stop, she was going to hurt herself. And you know what? She stopped. Just like that, she stopped. Her head was right up against the door, and she had that long black hair hanging down in front of her face, and then she started swaying back and forth, like she was drunk or something."

"Long black hair?" I asked.

"Yeah. I almost forgot about that. Long black hair."

"Then," said Darrell, "I got there with the food. She didn't look right at all, and I figured, sick, or drunk, or maybe even hāpai." His face brightened. *That's* why I got the crackers and poi. Good hāpai food for pregnant women. He shot a glance at his brother and they winked. "You never know when you gon' come across one hāpai lady. So I asked her if she was, but she neva' say nothin.' So I hand her the crackers and poi—I figure, no harm, right?

"And then, I swear, we both watched her. She stood up straight and started to fall back, and we caught her." They were excited to the point of tears, and were both silent for a minute.

Jason picked up the story. "Warm, flesh and blood, yeah?" Darrell nodded.

"So anyway, we caught her. Then her head snapped back and all her long hair fell back from her face...you tell him."

Darrell, sad now, seeming a bit frightened, said, "The thing is.... She never *had* one face!" We stood nervously on the pavement now, all feeling like truant teenagers.

As if to break the spell, they pulled me gently back toward the side exit. "See? Right there."

There was a huge dent in the door, one that might have been made by a rock, or a delivery truck. "I tell you," said the older brother, "we only saw that the next day. That night, we just got the hell outta here as fast as we could!"

The bus driver was beeping the horn, something he rarely does, so I thanked the brothers, and we gave each other the shaka sign. We boarded the bus, and I was suddenly a confused leader wondering privately if the whole world was haunted.

Dear Keone

The lookout at Nu'uanu Pali is appropriately named; quite literally, it means "cool heights of the cliffs." Those of you who have been there really don't need the translation.

The Pali was formed by Keaomelemele, a daughter of the gods and a kumu hula, who stood one day at the top of Waolani, the site of the lookout, and began an oli—a chant with one breath and no dance. Her voice was powerful enough to crumble a portion of the Ko'olau mountains so that they fell away, leaving the Nu'uanu Pali.

The Pali is filled with mana, and is also the site of Kamehameha's final victory before becoming king of all Hawai'i. Thousands of his enemies fell to their deaths during the battle.

Now it's one of the most popular tourist attractions on O'ahu. But for some, it serves a darker purpose; people sometimes commit suicide by jumping from it, as Kamehameha's enemies did centuries ago. Anyone who jumps off the Pali, after falling about a hundred feet, will strike a rock that juts out from the cliff. There have been a few—not many—survivors of the jump.

An emergency worker I know—for whom profiling brings a bit of sanity to her job—believes there is such a thing as a typical jumper—one she calls "Dear Keone."

"It goes like this," she told me. "It's usually a young local guy. He gets a letter from his girlfriend that goes something like this: 'Dear Keone, I'm sorry, but I love Kalani, and I can't see you anymore'—or some such. Sometimes the letter says 'a hui hou'— till we meet again. Bad joke."

This never made the news, but it really happened. A woman called her boyfriend—a guy we'll call George—and asked him to meet her at the Pali Lookout that night. She'd just discovered that he was married with three kids. "If you don't show up," she threatened, "I'll call your wife and tell her everything."

Helpless, George agreed. He parked his car, got out, and found her standing on the wall of the lookout, very close to the edge of the cliff, with a gun to her head. He ran toward her as fast as he could, and was blindsided by someone. He fell to the ground. And then he heard a gunshot. Knowing he had failed, he screamed, "No-o-o-o!"

George slowly got up, shook his head to clear it, and saw a giant of a man, a Hawaiian warrior, blocking his way. He was seven feet tall, wearing a simple malo, with a shark-tooth spear in his right hand.

At the same time, George heard screeching tires, and saw several squad cars. Four or five cops emerged, guns drawn, flashlights beaming. He opened his mouth to warn them about the warrior, but as he watched the cops run past him, he saw nothing.

The police surrounded the girl, and it appeared she was still alive; George heaved a sigh of relief. One was holding her by the shoulders, talking patiently and slowly to her.

One of the cops got up slowly and walked toward George, who was still on his knees. He stood over George, hands on his hips. "That girl," he said, "was gonna kill you."

George looked up at him, and for a minute the policeman seemed as large as the warrior. He mumbled something incoherent. The cop squatted down, at eye level with George.

"She had a gun, pointed right at you," he said, calmly and evenly. "Two bullets. One for you, one for her. Looks like we got here in time."

George nodded, and managed to blurt out a garbled "thanks." He was still dazed. But as the girl was led away and the cops left, he knew she'd intended to shoot him, then herself, and that she was not about to share him with anyone. If eternity was in the cards, she'd thought, they'd be in it together.

A day or so later, George was almost normal, but he needed to know about the warrior. His grandmother, a feisty old soul who kept the family records as accurately as a bookkeeper, was the only person he could turn to.

The old woman consulted her books. "The battle at Nuʻuanu. Ah, here it is." She looked up sharply at her grandson. "One of our ancestors," she said, "fought there. But he fought against Kamehameha, on the Maui side of the army." She set the book aside and glanced out her window.

"He was so brave. He fought as many of Kamehameha's warriors as he could, and then he was killed. Kamehameha himself ordered that he be given a warrior's funeral."

And then, suddenly, George's grandmother slapped him on the face with the back of her hand, stinging his cheek. He stood up, angry and hurt.

"What was *that* for, Tūtū?"

The grandmother's voice was cold and sharp. "That ancestor saved your life. You cannot see? That girl would have killed you if he hadn't knocked you down.

"And I tell you something else. The story you told me—if I had that gun right now, I'd shoot your ʻolos off myself!"

George said nothing, and left. For some reason, the story never made the news, something neither the police department or the newspapers can quite figure out. George's wife and kids never discovered a thing..

And George resumed his life, his grandmother always silently behind him, armed, and he was as faithful a husband and father as could ever be.

Where is the Light?

Her name was Persiphone Tengura, and she called herself Percy. Ever since she was a child, she had had the gift of second sight. Her parents understood that and taught her to nurture the gift and, most importantly, to use it wisely.

Every so often, she would meet a kindred spirit, and she would be revitalized, her quiet belief made even stronger. This is how we met.

Her son was one of my students, and as I came to know them both, we found that we had much in common. She lived in a haunted house on top of Hawai'i Nui Ridge, and she once told me of nightmarchers who would, every now and then, cut a path through her living room.

But her most memorable encounter took place not in Hawai'i, but in New York, in the middle of Manhattan. Her son had entered a national yo-yo competition, and it ended early on their first day there. She took him to stay with friends so she could do some sightseeing by herself.

She hadn't walked more than a few blocks when she saw a long line of people, all walking toward a brilliant light, and she knew immediately what it meant. No one else on the street noticed the line of souls, which extended back several blocks.

Now Percy had seen the light many times, and each time was even more awed by its beauty and power. She entered a state of religious rapture, abruptly interrupted when someone tapped on the back of her shoulder.

She turned and saw a young Middle Eastern man, dressed like a Mormon missionary—in a long, white-sleeved shirt with a black tie and black slacks. What jarred the symmetry of his appearance was a backpack he held in front, against his chest.

Suddenly, Percy realized that the backpack contained a bomb. She hid her terror well, and had enough sense not to show any fear at all. After all, the man did look lost.

"Can you help me?" he asked. His English was flawless.

"Sure," said Percy, mustering up enthusiasm.

"My mission is complete," said the man. "I'm looking for the light. Can you help me find it?"

Percy was a bit nervous now, knowing what she knew about the light and about the man, for she suddenly knew who he was. She pointed toward the procession. "Right there—where the people are lining up."

"Thank you," replied the man. Percy watched as he ran toward the light without taking a place in line. When he came close to the light, it turned dark, then black, and would not let him through.

He returned to Percy, tears in his eyes. And she noticed that his eyes had turned pitch-black. "My mission is completed," he said again. "I must find the light. Help me find it." He began repeating himself, and then wandered off, still muttering.

Percy decided to forego any sightseeing, went back to her hotel room, and stayed there the rest of the day. She told me that it was then that she realized that nothing that haunted her home in Hawai'i could have been as frightening as what she had seen, and that she would have given anything then to have been there.

The Red Curtain

One day in May of '02, a seven-year-old girl was killed in a hit-and-run on the 16th Avenue Bridge in Kaimukī. Her ghost was stuck on the bridge, unable to find her way home. Occasionally, she would approach pedestrians on the bridge to ask them for help, and when they asked where her house was, she'd point to the mauka side of the bridge.

I've found that pedestrians are, by and large, Good Samaritans at heart, and they were more than happy to help. But when they did, she would disappear at the end of the bridge, right before their eyes. There's much more to this story, but I'll tell you all about it later. Suffice it to say that the bridge was haunted.

And because it was haunted, I would, from time to time, take a group to the bridge. On one of these days, I met a nineteen-year-old Samoan, from Upolu—a newcomer. He was at least twice my height and size, but humble and very, very quiet. Other members of the group shot videos and took pictures; one girl even brought a dousing rod, which made her shriek as it moved by itself and pointed straight down. The boy, meanwhile, hadn't said a word all day. He had no camera. And he seemed very preoccupied.

We went to Zippy's in our van, for dinner and decompression. The members were a chatty lot, and they reviewed the footage while they ate, just in case something showed up. For all practical intents and purposes, I wasn't there anymore.

Then the Samoan boy tapped me on the shoulder and motioned for me to follow him outside. We left, unnoticed, and he stood next to the van. And I knew I would learn what had been troubling him all afternoon.

"Last week," he said, "I was hired over there"— he motioned toward a large movie theater. "An usher. Gotta make money to send home to my family in Samoa. See, I got a U.H. football scholarship, but it's not enough. I do what I can." He shrugged, his face almost without expression.

"First day I work there, they told me the old general manager quit, but nobody knows why, you know? Anyway, I'm working the closing shift—four in the afternoon to midnight. Everybody was teasing me, like this—'Oooo!!! Theater Numbah 6! Numbah 6!' It was kind of funny at first, but it really bugged me after a while, and I guess they could see I was getting mad so they left me alone.

"Anyway, a little after midnight, I went into number 6. The surprise—man! Whole damn theater full with toilet paper! All the seats the floor, all over the screen.

"I guess it was kind of an initiation, and suddenly I had to laugh. Then I started to pick up the mess when something caught my eye. There were red curtains against the wall, and they were moving. Looked to me like somebody was standing behind the curtain and poking out the material with their hands or their feet. So I ran right up to the curtain and punched, one time, just to let the guy know.

"And you know what? I hit nothing but solid concrete. Hooo, the pain! Good thing for me nothing broken, but the pain! I got so made I pulled down the curtain. Nobody there—how you figure? I could swear I saw somebody.

"I tried to cool off little bit. Then I ran out to get the others, and I told them to follow me back inside. They all looked around, and everybody was real quiet. One guy told me to look around very carefully. So I did, but I didn't see anything.

"Finally, one of the girls told me, 'No more red curtains here, you! Only green. Always green curtains! Jeez!' And I looked around, and she was right, Green curtains around the screen and at the exit.

"So I ran to the pay phone outside the lobby and I called my uncle in Lāʻie. I told him come there and bless the place before I go back, I don't care what time it is.

"You see, in Samoa, some of us believe that you are not supposed to leave your village at night, because if you encounter a spirit, you will not return home alive. And after what I saw, I'm not taking any chances, you know?

"My uncle can't come down; car's broken. So I quit the job right there. And that's my story." He seemed lighter and calmer. "I'm glad I got it off my chest. You were the right person to tell this story to."

All I could say was "Don't mention it."

He shook my hand warmly, the other hand cupped over my right, and walked back to Zippy's. The conversation was light and lively, and everybody went home happy.

Obon

Most people think of ghosts around Halloween time, in October, but this is a Western idea. In Hawai'i, our ghosts don't pay much attention to tradition, and they tend to operate outside the box. Whether they do this out of whimsy or spite is anyone's guess.

In 2002, for example, there was an unusually active time for ghosts between mid-July and mid-August. This is not as uncommon as it seems, since it coincides with the Japanese celebration of the dead. For those in the Japanese 'ohana who believe in *obake*—or ghosts—the time is known as *Obon.*

Once there were three girls who cut summer school during the second week in July to see a Brad Pitt movie. The theater was in a shopping center, and the oldest girl, whose name was Tess, realized that she had to find a bathroom. Her friends walked her to a bookstore. Tess was edgy and impatient.

"Wait," she said. There's no bathroom here. This is a bookstore."

"Will you be quiet?" her friends told her. "We're trying to show you where it is." They headed for an escalator, passed it, and headed round the corner to a winding hallway. "Over there," said her friends. "We'll wait for you here."

She found the bathroom. She went to the sink to wash her hands and saw, standing there, a woman who looked like a bar hostess. She was wearing a cheap black dress with sequins, too low at the top and way too high on the skirt. Her shoulder straps were thin. The woman was brushing her short curly hair wildly in front of the mirror, with such force that she actually tore hair off her scalp and drew blood. Tess was horrified, shaking, and moving very slowly around the woman and edging toward the door. But as she reached the door, the woman slammed both of her hands down on the bathroom sink, and it sounded like an explosion.

Tess screamed and turned to run out of the bathroom, but in her blind panic ran into the wall instead. She tore a muscle in her right shoulder and her forehead was bruised and aching. And yet somehow she could not resist looking back as she found the door and ran out. The woman had pulled her hair away from her face. She had no nose, no mouth, and her face had no contour or shape whatsoever. She only had a pair of eyes.

And they were looking right at Tess.

Her scream was loud enough to scare half the shopping center, and probably did. A security guard guided her out and sat her down on a bench with her two friends. When she had regained enough balance to tell her story, her friends were horrified. But the security guard was less than sympathetic, and his face was cold.

"Look" he said. "If you see anything in this mall—ghosts, whatever—just keep it to yourself." The three girls looked at him in stunned silence.

He went on, his voice flat, betraying a hint of anger. "All of us guards have heard this faceless ghost story, from every business in the mall, and the owners are blaming *us* for it. So if you seen anything, anything at all, say nothing. Understand? It's bad for business."

Tess and her two friends never saw the movie. They made it back to school in time for social studies. The topic for that day was local culture, specifically *Obon*. None of the three slept too well that night, and they took pains to be in class every day.

Obake

We're reaching the end of the book, and I thought I'd tell you a bit about myself. I'm Hawaiian, and I grew up in Waipahu during the Seventies, when it was still a sugar town. Many of my friends were Japanese, and as we grew up together, we would eat at the same restaurants together after school and attend the same karate class in the evenings. The *dojo* was run by Mr. Miyaji, whom we called *Sensei.* It's a Japanese word that means teacher or master.

Japanese traditions are part of life all over Hawai'i, and Waipahu was no exception. These traditions include a belief in ghosts, known as *Obake.* My friends told me that their parents and grandparents brought the ghosts with them to keep them company during dark and lonely nights on the plantation. I think they were only half-kidding. For there is nothing quite like a good *Obake* story spun by a Japanese grandparent.

And as we grew older, and thought we had outgrown the grandparents, we would watch movies at the old Toyo Theater. I can't speak for anyone else, but nothing produced now—no matter how slick, or realistic—can compare to the old Japanese *Obake* films. They were low-budget thrillers, but they scared the living daylights out of me. Come to think of it, they still do.

I'm digressing a bit. When I was a kid attending *dojo*, I once noticed a statue of a demon—or a figure with a demon's face—attached to a muscular human body in a karate pose. I summoned up the courage to ask *Sensei* Miyaji about it. He told me it was the god of karate, and I let it go at that.

But one night, after class, *Sensei* asked me if I could go upstairs to fetch his *gi*—the shirt worn for karate—and handed me his keys. I found his uniform right where he said it would be and returned downstairs. Then I heard something I will never forget. All the lights were off by now, but I heard a grunt inside the studio where we'd practiced barely an hour before. I couldn't resist peeking in. I saw the god of karate moving, practicing, doing *kata*—forms, warm-up exercises for combat—and grunting. I remember like I do yesterday, but my mind is blank on what happened next. I obviously got out of there and went home, but I don't know when or how I got there. It gives me chicken skin to think about it now, years later.

Truth be told, I simply put it out of my mind for a long time. When I turned eighteen, I became a practicing Buddhist of a branch known as *Sokka Gakkai*, and remain a member after twenty-five years. My wife's been a member even longer than I have, and our daughter was born into it.

For me as a Hawaiian, this form of Buddhism is very, very close to the very first religion of my people—long before the introduction of the ali'i class system and human sacrifice. It teaches a reverence and a kind of peace with the world, difficult to describe in words. Suffice it to say that when I first learned the story of the faceless woman, I felt prepared culturally. I wasn't prepared for it in my gut, though, and it would be a while before I would learn the full story behind the legend.

The Summer Yukata

This is the final story, and it took place during a summer long gone, in a KaimukI and a Wai'alae that live now only in old black and white photographs on the walls of restaurants and homes.

The people who knew the story firsthand are long gone; their time on this earth marked on gravestones and their friends' memories. The legends may fade when they pass on, but they never disappear.

There is, for example, the legend of the faceless woman of Wai'alae. I heard the story when I was a kid, and believed it, and as I matured, I began to dismiss it as an urban legend. I had graduated from Waipahu and its country ways and moved to Honolulu, and city folk, we were taught, make up ghost stories out of whole cloth to entertain themselves and to fool strangers.

I mentioned a summer long gone. It was actually fairly recent—'02, to be precise—but I will always remember it as a summer where the distant past wrestled the present and won, making it another time altogether. This'll take some explaining.

I had a group, and we toured Wai'alae, and talked about the faceless woman. We were standing at the foot of an old graveyard, and I began to weave a tale of the first known hauntings—they took place at the old Wai'alae Drive-Inn—and mentioned that they had even been reported in the newspaper by a young reporter named Bob Krauss. I was having a grand old time. Then a voice, old but firm, came from the back of the group.

"That was *not* the first time somebody saw her."

I looked over the crowd. "Excuse me?" I said.

"Somebody saw her before then." She was an elderly Japanese woman who stepped forward slowly. She was neither arrogant nor humble, a matter-of-fact woman wearing shorts and a pink top. Her hair was short and I remember it had been dyed a kind of faded red. I remember thinking to myself, old lady hair, but said nothing.

"I don't like to interrupt," she said. "But you're not quite right. Somebody saw her before they built the drive-in. It was me."

Suddenly she seemed out-of-place, a party-crasher, an anomaly. But everyone turned to listen to her, and so did I.

"See, she was still alive back then. I remember it was the first part of the year, 1957. Her husband came from Japan, and he came from one rich family. He never told her, because he was proud and wanted to make his own way. Real hardhead." She shook her head in disgust.

"Anyway, they had five kids. But the poor guy, he died suddenly, around age thirty-five, and suddenly, she finds out she's inherited all his money. Overnight, she was rich. Too rich, too soon, if you ask me.

"She moved to some fancy neighborhood—I forget which—and she started ignoring her kids. Same time, she buys all kind fancy stuff—furniture, nice car, jewelry. But the thing I remember was a kimono—daytime kimono, a *Yukata*—made by hand, with the fancy *obi*. Now here's the funny thing." She had everyone's attention now, and whether I liked it or not, she had mine as well.

"She wore that kimono all over town. All the time. And Hawai'i so hot daytime, nobody dress like that. One day I ran into her by Mō'ili'ili, and—I'm not shy—I went right up to her and said, 'How come you wear kimono. So hot!

"You know what she said? Even this day I don't believe it. She says, 'Because I can afford to.' I still don't believe it." She shook her head, as though to clear it of the memory.

"Anyway," she went on, "next thing you know she's starting to gamble. *Hanafuda* games with a lot of other Japanese ladies who dress all fancy and act high makamaka! They not playing penny-ante. They playing for big bucks. And all the while she doesn't know or care where the five kids are.

"The kids got angry, and they banded together. One of them had a friend in school who was the shadiest lawyer in town. Somehow, the guy managed to talk the woman into making him trustee—he must have been a smooth buggah—and let him hold the money in trust for her and the kids. I figure she must have agreed because she felt a little guilty, but the spending and the gambling continued, and the parties.

"One day, she gets up, goes to the bank, and finds out that there's no money there. She calls her stockbroker, and everything's been sold. Pretty soon, no mortgage money. And she finds out that the lawyer, along with the kids, made an arrangement. He took a healthy percentage as a trustee, but gave the rest to the kids, who split it evenly and moved away, every one of them. All on the Mainland.

"Pretty soon it's obvious to her *hanafuda* friends. At first they're—you know—so sorry, and all that. And before you know it, they not speaking to her. Kicked her out of the group. All her new friends disappear overnight, just like the cash and the kids.

"One time, I heard, she went back to them in tears still wearing her kimono, which was about all she had. One of them stands up to her and says, real makamaka like, 'You shame your dead husband. You have no honor. You are no longer a part of our group. You have lost face!"

"And no one saw her for quite a while. Then, about a week before they opened the Wai'alae Drive-Inn, I was in bed one night. We lived close by. I woke up—must have been about two in the morning—and I hear this crying, real pitiful, right outside the house. I went to the front door and opened it just a little bit. I didn't see anything, but I heard a woman's voice. She was crying out names—later, I found out, her childrens: 'Yasuooooo! Dai-Chaaaan! Yoshikooooo! Midoriiiii! Takemiiiiiiii!'

"Like I said, I'm not shy. Oh, and I forgot to tell you I was just married too. Anyway, I was just about to open the front door when my husband comes down. He says to me, '*Urusai!*' which means be quiet. I grabbed him to try to get him from running outside, because I was getting scared. I think he was scared too, because he started yelling at me.

'Lemme go!' I gotta tell that lady to be quiet! She waking up the whole neighborhood!'

"Sakae," I said, "No. Leave her alone."

"'Why?,'" he demanded.

"Because," I told him, "she's not human anymore. *Obake.* Look."

"We both looked up the road to see a woman wearing a *yukata*—a white one. No *'obi* around the waist; it was open. The woman's hair was black, very long, went all the way to her ankles. And she had her arms stretched out. We watched her for a long time, walking slowly, like a dream. And then she stopped, and turned around and headed toward our house. My husband and I saw that she wasn't walking at all. The woman was floating. She had no feet. No feet—can you imagine? And her hair was in front of her face.

"Sakae and I just stood there, I don't know why. Then the woman spoke. 'I have no honor,' over and over again, and she was crying, and then she said, 'I have lost face.'

"Then she parts her hair with her hands and pulled it back one time! Somehow, I knew who she was. She had no face. No face at all." The woman was staring at the ground now. "No face."

We were all silent, and unnerved. She continued talking. I think we all knew that she had to get it out.

"Year after that, I start to hear about this faceless ghost at the Wai'alae Drive-Inn. But I can't say anything. I know she's not trying to scare anybody. It's like—it's like she's stuck forever and has to show anybody who will look that she is a woman with no honor. A woman who has lost face."

She paused, as though catching her breath, and then said, "I saw her one more time, same year. Right about the end of the *Obon* Festivals at the Mō'ili'ili Hongwanji. We were all dancing and having a good time. And just for one second, I saw her, and I swear she was dancing too. But she was moving her hands real strange, and it looked like she was pointing at the old Kumula'e pond. And then I remember that during *Obon* you not supposed to go by any pond or river, 'cause that's where all the dead people with no family to pray for them go. And if you go close to the water, maybe they come out, drag you in and drown you."

We stood very still and silent for a long time; we could have passed for statues. Then I asked the group to step away from the cemetery and we moved, slowly first, then quickly, to our cars. We stopped somewhere to compare notes, but nobody had anything to say, so we said goodbye to each other. Then I noticed the woman wasn't there.

"Where'd the old lady go?" I asked. We looked all around and couldn't find hide nor hair of her. Now the thing you have to understand is that where we were, there was no way she could have run off without someone noticing. I shrugged, which is my way of whistling in the dark when nothing can be explained.

I can speak only for myself, but for a long time after that I'd get jumpy at the sight of anyone dressed in white.

There's a footnote to this story—a forty-eight-old one, which is what I mean about past and present colliding (I often wonder what happens when past, present and future meet at the same intersection and run the stop sign, but that's for another story at another time).

The first report of the Wai'alae haunting was on May 17, 1958, a Saturday. There was a movie at the drive-in that night. Some say it was one of those Doris Day-Rock Hudson flicks. Others remember Gregory Peck. You guess.

Father of Invention

He was my friend and mentor, and I miss Glen Grant every day. And it seems that he is still part of all my days. I may mention him myself, or I will meet someone who knew him and his work. And my own work is really Glen's legacy. For me, he's still very much here, something I find reassuring.

He passed away on June 19, 2003, at 2:00 A.M. As he himself knew, this is a particularly busy hour for Hawaiian spirits. It was something he often mentioned during his own ghost tours. For Glen, the time of his passing was both ironic and, perhaps in its own way, fitting—if it had to happen at all.

He was a Jewish kid from Hollywood who came here in the Seventies to study American history. He didn't know that his arrival would be, in its own way, an historical event. He became a master storyteller, well-known and respected throughout Hawai'i and the world, and he spent thirty years collecting stories about ghosts and spirits, which he took care to publish. He also created a fictional detective from the Thirties named McDougal—Honolulu's answer to Sam Spade. Glen's imagination was boundless. And then he left us, on a starry night.

He did not go willingly. For Glen, there was still so much to be done and discovered, and at least three more books to publish, and this, perhaps, angered him most as the end approached. He finally resigned himself to the fact that there would be no more stories. He lifted the veil which separates this world from the next, and he joined the procession of souls toward Ka'ena Point. Then he climbed a rock—one known as leina-a-ka-'uhane, and leapt into Milu, the netherworld.

Many people have asked me, half jokingly and half in earnest, whether I have seen Glen's ghost. I have not. But I remember his telling me that he would come back from the dead and keep doing his ghost tours. Some of you have been lucky enough to accompany Glen on his tours, and if you join mine, you will find mine very different from his. The reason for this is simple. I don't want to run into him some night. It would be discourteous to my oldest and dearest friend.

So I honor his legacy in my own way. I write books like this one. And at night, I take people out to the darkest corners of the island and I scare the living daylights out of them.

About the Author

Robert Lopaka Kapanui is a teacher's assistant at Kawaiahaʻo School and a teller of ghost stories. A hula dancer, member of the Koʻolau Lodge of F&AM, and of the Royal Order of Kamehameha, Kapanui has been featured in two independent films—*The Red Hibiscus*, and *2*—for Pacific Islanders in Communication and Pennybacker Creative, LLC. He is currently directing another PIC short film titled *A Pagan Tattooed Savage*.

His most precious moments are spent with his wife and daughter.